THE WORLD'S BEST DOG-WALKER

Written by Pam Zollman
Illustrated by Tim Raglin

STECK-VAUGHN
ELEMENTARY · SECONDARY · ADULT · LIBRARY

A Harcourt Classroom Education Company

www.steck-vaughn.com

Contents

Need someone to walk your dog? Call Abby Simmons World's BEST Dog-Walker 454-9765 Reasonable

CHAPTER 1

Broken Bike

"Look out!" I yelled. "I can't stop!"

My brakes weren't working again. I was speeding faster and faster down the street on a runaway bicycle. I pushed back on the pedals hard, but nothing happened. That meant the chain had come off, or it had broken. Either way, I was in trouble.

Directly ahead of me, a woman was walking her German shepherd. If she didn't move, I'd run over her and turn her into a pancake with tire marks. Actually, she'd look more like a waffle.

"Get out of the way!" I shouted. "My brakes won't work!"

The lady looked back at me, and her mouth dropped open in surprise. I shot toward her like a race car aiming for the finish line. But instead of jumping out of the way, she froze in panic.

I tried to swerve, but my back wheel skidded. Luckily, I missed the woman and her dog, too. Unluckily, the bike hit the curb, and I landed hard on the grass.

"Are you hurt?" the woman asked.

"No," I said, sitting up, "but I sure was scared." I brushed grass and leaves off my shirt.

Her German shepherd licked my cheek and wagged his tail. I love dogs, so I petted him. He

reminded me of Cody, the German shepherd that we had when I was little. He looked fierce, but he was very gentle. He was the best pillow I ever had. We'd curl up on the floor and watch TV together. I was so small and Cody was so big that I thought he looked like a horse! Cody died of old age a long time ago, but I still missed him.

"Well, I'm glad you're all right," the woman said and tugged on the German shepherd's leash. "Come on, Duke. Let's finish our walk. I have to go shopping. Seems like I never have time any more for a good walk." The two of them went down the street.

My best friend, Bird, skidded to a stop beside me. Her real name is Bernadette, but her older sister shortened it to Bird when Bird was just a baby. Now everyone calls her that.

Bird is tall and slim. When she rides her bike the right way, her knees hit the handle bars. Usually she sticks her knees out sideways.

"Abby, are you okay?" she asked.

"Yeah." I stood up. "I'm glad I didn't hit that lady and her dog. But something's wrong with my brakes."

"Something's wrong with your whole bike," said Bird. She held up my broken chain.

"Oh, no," I groaned. "Now I'll have to buy a new one."

Bird laughed. "You need to buy a new bike."

I snorted. "Look who's talking. Your bike is way too small."

She grinned. "Look at yours. It looks like a patchwork quilt of bicycle parts."

"Okay," I said, "we both need new bikes. But we don't have enough money to buy them. In fact, I don't have any money to even fix my old one, and Mom says we can't afford it right now."

"Maybe we could earn some money," Bird suggested.

"How?" I asked.

Bird scratched her head and thought. "My dad says the trick is to offer a service that other people want. It should be something they need to

do but don't want to do. That way, they're willing to pay someone else to do it."

"Like what?" I asked.

She rubbed her chin and thought for a moment more. "Washing cars?"

"Too wet," I said.

"Yard work?" Bird suggested.

I wrinkled my nose. "Too sweaty."

"Baby-sitting?" Bird sounded a bit frustrated.

"Definitely not," I said. "My mom thinks *I* need a baby-sitter."

As I picked up my bike, I gazed down the street at the German shepherd. That triggered an idea. "I know! We could walk dogs!"

"Walk dogs?" Bird looked at me like I had just told her I was really an alien.

"Yeah," I said, "for people who can't do it themselves."

She shook her head. "It'd never work."

"Sure it would," I said eagerly. "That lady said she didn't have enough time to walk Duke. I bet she'd pay someone to do it for her."

"We don't have any experience," she protested.

"Sure we do," I said. "I love dogs and have lots of experience. I know all about feeding and taking care of them. We had a German shepherd just like Duke. After he died, we got a pug from the animal shelter. Mom named him Winston. She said he looked like Winston Churchill, that famous English guy."

Winston loved to chase tennis balls and eat. I'd let him lick stamps and envelopes for me. He liked the taste of glue.

Mom said that Winston liked the taste of everything. He had only been with us for a few years when he developed heart problems. I cried when Winston died. I still missed him. Mom had talked about getting another dog, but right now we couldn't afford one.

The more I thought about walking other people's dogs, the more excited I got. It would be fun taking someone else's dog for a walk, since I couldn't have one of my own. Bird and I could have a dog-walking business together. We'd both make money to buy new bikes.

Then Bird said something that surprised me. "Since you're the one with all the experience," she said, "you do it."

"What do you mean?" I asked, puzzled.

She frowned. "You can walk dogs
if you want to, but not me. I don't
want any part of it."

"But Bird!" I protested. "It's so easy! You just
snap the leash onto the dog, and away you go.
Dogs love to go for walks. It's a great way to make
money."

"For you, Abby," she insisted, "but not for me."

That wasn't the answer I wanted to hear from
my best friend.

2

Big Baby

Well, I had to admit that Bird hurt my feelings. I couldn't figure out why she didn't want to start a dog-walking business with me. Did she hate dogs? Was she afraid of them? Was she mad at me because I didn't like her money-making ideas?

I decided not to worry about it any more. Maybe when I got the business going, Bird would join in. I hoped so. Ever since she'd moved across the street from me, we'd always done everything together.

When I told Mom the next day, she said my business was a good idea. "What are you going to call it?" she asked.

"I don't know yet," I admitted. "I thought about calling it Abby and Bird's Dog-Walking Service."

11

Mom smiled. "That sounds like a good name."

"The problem is that I want Bird to be a part of it," I explained, "but she doesn't want to. She didn't say why, either."

"Maybe she'll change her mind," Mom said. "You know, I've never heard of a service like this, but you'll be good at it."

I laughed. "If no one's ever done it before, then when I do it, I'll be the best!"

"The world's best," Mom agreed.

"That's the name!" I said excitedly. I hugged Mom and danced around the kitchen table. "World's Best Dog-Walker. After all, no one loves dogs more than I do!"

"You were wonderful with Cody and Winston," Mom said. "And Bird will join you when she's ready. Just wait and see."

I hoped Mom was right. Bird and I hadn't talked since the day before. I missed her already.

Mom gave me paper, and I used colored markers to make flyers for my business. Hoping to get lots of customers, I put them up all around the neighborhood.

On Monday I got a phone call from Mrs. Garza after school. She'd seen my flyer and was very interested.

"Is this Abby Simmons, the dog-walker?" she asked.

"Yes, ma'am," I said.

"You say you're the best?" she asked.

Need someone to walk your dog? Call Abby Simmons World's BEST Dog-Walker 454-9765 Reasonable

"Yes, ma'am," I said again. "I'm the world's best."

"Good," she said. "You're hired. Please come over right away. Baby will be waiting."

When I arrived, Mrs. Garza explained that she and her husband were too tired to walk Baby after working long hours, so Baby stayed cooped up inside all day.

"Baby loves to go for walks," she said. She handed me a leash with a gigantic bouncing ball attached. Actually the bouncing ball was a huge, six-month-old, long-legged Great Dane puppy.

Some baby! I think he weighed almost as much as I did. Baby was so excited that he almost knocked me over trying to get out the front door.

Once outside, though, Baby didn't want to go for a walk. Oh no, not Baby. Instead he chased a squirrel up a tree. Then he chased a cat, but the cat boxed his nose. Baby even leaped after the butterflies.

He sniffed everything from mailboxes to trees to dandelions. The dandelions made him sneeze. Then he sat down and scratched at a flea. After all that, we had only gotten as far as the front sidewalk! Mrs. Garza was wrong. Baby loved doing everything *except* walking.

Baby sprawled at my feet and licked my ankle. I tugged on the leash, trying to get him to walk. He jumped up on me, almost knocking me over. Then he raced around me, wrapping me up like a present with the leash. This was going to be a very long walk.

I sat on the ground and tried to figure out how to get Baby to do the simple job of walking around the block. He nibbled on my shoes, then threw back his head and howled.

"That dog sounds like a train," a voice said.

I turned around and smiled when I saw Bird. Maybe she'd changed her mind about the dog-walking business.

Pointing to Baby, I said, "That train derailed me." The puppy leaped up, lunged at Bird, and made excited yipping noises.

Bird backed out of Baby's reach. "Go away, you crazy dog!" she yelled.

I yanked Baby back toward me. "Come on, Bird. Help me with the dog-walking business. I'm calling it World's Best Dog-Walker."

"No way," Bird said.

"Why not?" I asked. "You're not afraid of dogs, are you?"

She hesitated a moment, then admitted, "I've never been around dogs very much. We never had one because my mom is allergic to them."

"Then you're not really afraid of them. You're just not used to them," I said.

"I don't think I'd ever get used to a dog like that one." Bird took two more steps back.

"Baby will grow out of a lot of his wildness," I explained. "Plus he needs someone to train him. The first thing he needs to learn is how to walk on a leash. I just can't figure out how to teach him."

Bird smiled. "You need a carrot and a stick."
She ran to her house. A few minutes later, she
returned with a fishing pole and a bag with a
ham sandwich in it.

"The sandwich is the carrot, and the fishing
pole is the stick," she explained. She tied the
fishing line to the sandwich and slung the pole
over her shoulder.

I laughed. "Now I see. The sandwich is bait."
Bird kept the sandwich just out of Baby's reach.
The puppy trotted behind her,
his eyes on the bait. All I had
to do was hold on to the
leash and keep Baby
from trying to grab
the sandwich.

At the end of our walk, Bird and I shared the ham sandwich with the puppy. Bird sat just far enough away that Baby couldn't reach her. When we finished eating, the puppy licked my fingers clean. He was sleepy, and his tummy was full. Now he looked really sweet, not at all like the wild thing he'd been.

"That was a great idea, Bird," I said. "Who would have thought of using a fishing pole to teach a dog to walk on a leash? Not me!"

Bird grinned. "Glad to have been of service."

I grinned back. "Boy, I'm glad you're part of the dog-walking business now. I can really use your help."

"No," Bird said, "I'm not part of your business, Abby. All I did today was help a friend. I still don't like dogs."

That wasn't what I wanted to hear, but I didn't know what to do about it.

CHAPTER 3

Chasing Clover

Good news! Mrs. Garza was so pleased that she told her neighbor about my dog-walking service. Mr. Thorn called me to come over right away to walk Clover.

I arrived at his house a few minutes later. Mr. Thorn said, "I understand that there's no one better at walking dogs than you."

I beamed. "That's right."

"Are you fast?" he asked.

"Fast?" I repeated.

"At running," he added.

I shrugged. "I guess so."

"Good!" Mr. Thorn pointed to the braces on his legs. "It's hard for me to exercise Clover, and she loves to go for a walk."

I petted Clover. "You called the right person."

Clover was a cute little dog that looked like a cocker spaniel. She had big brown eyes and long, silky ears. Mr. Thorn snapped the leash onto Clover's collar. Her stubby tail wagged so hard that her whole body shook. Boy was she happy to go for a walk!

I opened the door, and that twenty-pound dog changed from a quivering furball into a heat-seeking missile. We shot down the steps and across the yard, with me barely hanging onto her leash.

Clover strained to run as fast as possible down the street. Yanking on the leash didn't slow her down a bit. Clover raced forward, her tongue

hanging out the side of her mouth, her ears flapping backwards. She almost pulled me off my feet. I think I swallowed a bug, yelling "Stop!"

Clover rounded the corner just as Bird came skating down the sidewalk. Clover missed her, but the dog made me crash into Bird. Bird and I fell in a heap on the grass.

The leash slipped out of my hand. Clover was free! She raced down the sidewalk like a kid running to the swimming pool on the first day of summer.

"Did you get the license plate of the truck that hit me?" Bird asked as she sat up.

"That wasn't a truck," I said, sitting up, too. "That was a dog named Clover."

Bird shook her head. "The dog's name is Clover. Why are we the ones rolling in it?" she asked.

"Maybe that's how she got her name," I said as I helped Bird stand up.

Bird looked around. "Where's Clover?"

The dog was out of sight. "Oh, no! I've got to find her!" I started running down the street.

Bird skated after me. About six houses down, I found Clover. Her leash had gotten tangled around a bush in someone's side yard.

It took some time to free Clover because she wouldn't stay still, but I finally got her untangled. Bird watched from what she thought was a safe distance. Once free from the bush, Clover wagged her whole body, wiggling up next to me.

"What's wrong with her?" Bird asked as she stared at Clover.

"Nothing," I replied. "She just wants to be petted."

"That's why she's shaking all over?" Bird looked doubtful and didn't come any closer.

"Yeah," I said. Clover rolled onto her back, pawing the air, so I scratched her stomach. "Why don't you try it?"

"Rolling in the clover with Clover?" Bird laughed and shook her head. "I don't think so. My stomach doesn't need scratching."

I rolled my eyes. "You know what I mean."

"Yeah, well, I still don't want to pet her." Then she changed the subject. "So how are you going to walk a dog who only likes to run at the speed of light?"

"I don't know," I admitted. "Until I met Clover, I thought I was pretty fast."

"I have an idea," Bird offered. She bent down and unlaced her skates. "Use these and maybe you can keep up with her."

"Hey, thanks! Great idea!" I took off my shoes and laced up Bird's skates. They were regular skates, like the ones I had at home.

"You can bring them to me later," Bird said. She picked up my shoes and headed home.

Taking a firm grip on the leash, I asked, "Clover, do you want to go for a wa—"

She didn't even let me finish my question. We were off! Clover pulled me on Bird's skates like a sled dog in Alaska. We went for blocks and blocks. Too bad we weren't in a race, because I know we would've won.

When I finally brought Clover home, she was worn out but happy. Mr. Thorn was happy. I got really happy as he counted out dollar bills into my hand.

I went to Bird's apartment and returned her skates. "Thanks," I said. "The skates worked like magic. Clover could go as fast as she wanted. All I had to do was stay vertical."

Bird laughed. "Hey, you're a good skater. That shouldn't have been a problem."

Grinning, I said, "You try it sometime."

Bird stopped laughing. "I told you I wasn't going to be part of your dog-walking business."

"There has to be a way to convince you," I told her.

"No way," she replied.

"But you keep coming up with great ideas," I protested.

She shook her head. "Forget it."

I couldn't forget it, but I didn't know what to do, either.

CHAPTER 4

Finicky Fifi

"Mr. Thorn told me about your dog-walking service," said the elderly voice on the phone. "He says you're the world's best. Is that true?"

"Yes, ma'am, Miss Strake," I replied.

"Only the best will do for Fifi," the old woman said. "She's a very special dog, you know."

"Yes, ma'am," I replied. "When would you like for me to come over?"

"Fifi could use some fresh air and sunshine. Come today at three," Miss Strake said. "And be prompt. Fifi doesn't like it if you're late."

"Uh, yes, ma'am." I'd heard rumors about the finicky Fifi.

Miss Strake was old and lived alone in a small house that needed painting and repairs. She spent all her money on her little dog. She had never married and had no children, unless you counted Fifi. Photos of the "special" white poodle decorated the inside of her house.

Miss Strake led me to Fifi's room. Pink poodle wallpaper covered the walls. Dog toys littered the floor. A pink water bowl and a white food bowl sat on their own pink-and-white flowered placemats. A cookie jar shaped like a poodle sat on one table.

In the middle of the room, Fifi lay sleeping on her own special oversized, overstuffed pink pillow. Around her neck she wore a rhinestone collar. The fake jewels glittered in the light. When we walked in, Fifi sat up and looked at us like a queen regarding her subjects.

"Are you awake, dumpling?" Miss Strake offered her a cookie shaped like a fire hydrant. Fifi nibbled on it as if she were very bored.

"Sweetie," Miss Strake cooed, "I want you to meet Abby. She's going to take you for a walk."

I smiled at the poodle, who did not smile back. Instead, she spit out the dog cookie.

Miss Strake opened the closet door, and inside I could see shelves full of dog food and dog treats. Tiny sweaters on tiny hangers hung on rods. Matching collars and leashes hung on hooks on the wall. I had never seen a closet so neat.

I'm pretty sure that Fifi had more clothes than I did. I know for sure that she had more toys! I was thinking seriously about learning how to bark and walk on all fours so that Miss Strake would adopt me.

Miss Strake clipped a rhinestone leash to Fifi's collar. I expected to see Fifi change from pillow potato to firecracker, as the other dogs had done when they realized they were going for a walk. Not Fifi. She merely yawned.

"Fresh air will be good for you, my love," Miss Strake told Fifi.

Fifi was not impressed. The elderly woman handed me the leash.

"Come on, Fifi," I said, tugging on her leash. "Time to exercise."

Fifi looked at me as if I were crazy. We were having language problems. Apparently Fifi didn't understand the word "exercise," and it was obvious she could certainly use some.

"Now sugar plum," Miss Strake urged, "you'll love it outside." Fifi yawned again and closed her eyes. Then she flopped down on the pillow.

I tugged again, harder this time. Fifi wasn't convinced. She locked her legs and tugged back. Gee, she was pretty strong for a poodle.

Miss Strake got out a treat from her pocket and dangled it in front of Fifi's nose. "Come on, Fifi baby. Go with Abby."

The dog didn't even sniff the treat. She was still unimpressed and still unconvinced. Finally I just did what any business person would do. I scooped up Fifi, leash and all, and headed out the front door. Boy was that poodle heavy!

I put her down on the sidewalk and tried again. I pulled on her leash and started walking. Wonder of wonders, she was following! All right! This was better. We were walking!

Then I looked back. Fifi wasn't walking after all. She was just trembling as I dragged her a few feet.

Fifi looked so sad, so frightened. She was shaking like the last leaf left on a tree in autumn. I sighed and sat down beside her.

"Hey Abby," Bird yelled from down the street. "What is that thing? A cotton ball with legs?"

"This is Fifi," I said when she got closer. "We're going for a walk."

Bird laughed. "Looks more like dog-sitting than dog-walking."

"I guess it's going to be more like dog-carrying," I said. "She refuses to walk. I don't think she gets much fresh air."

Still quivering, Fifi crawled into my lap. I rubbed her ears.

"Is she shaking because she wants to be petted?" Bird asked. "That's what Clover did."

"Yes," I said, "but it's not like Clover. Clover wiggled with excitement and wanted her tummy scratched because she was happy. Fifi wants me to pet her because she's scared."

"Scared?" Bird asked. "Of what?"

I shrugged, then told her how spoiled Fifi was. "She's a queen with her own throne room at home, but outside there's no throne."

"She has her own room?" Bird asked. "I don't even have my own room! I have to share with my sister."

"Don't forget her special pillow," I added. "It's better than mine."

"Wait a minute," Bird said. "I think I know what the problem is. I'll be right back." She raced off in the direction of her house.

When she came back a few minutes later, she was pulling a red wagon. "Go get her pillow," Bird said.

The pillow fit perfectly inside the wagon. Fifi fit the pillow perfectly. I just knew this would work. I pulled her around the neighborhood, with Bird following.

Fifi still shivered once in awhile, so I kept patting her head and reassuring her. Pulling that wagon was hard work. When I stopped to rest for a minute, Fifi wagged her cotton-ball tail and licked my face, as happy as any pampered pup I'd ever seen.

"Do you think Fifi would let me pet her?" Bird asked.

Surprised, I stared at Bird. "You really want to?"

"Yeah," she said. "I guess I feel sorry for her. She looks so scared."

"You like her because she's not wild at all," I observed.

"That *is* a plus," Bird said, grinning.

I stopped the wagon and watched Bird carefully place her hands on Fifi's head. Then she scratched behind the poodle's ears. Fifi thumped her tail, and I think both Bird and Fifi were smiling.

"Her fur's so soft," Bird said. "I thought it would feel rougher. I just don't know very much about dogs."

"It takes time," I replied, trying to encourage her.

"It would be easy to learn with Fifi," Bird said. She was still petting the chubby little poodle.

I decided to press my luck. "Look how well you two are getting along," I said. "Are you going to be part of my dog-walking service now?"

Bird shook her head and pulled her hand off Fifi. "No."

Rats!

CHAPTER 5

Perfect Partners

"How can you just say no like that?" I asked, truly confused. "I thought we were friends."

"It's simple," Bird answered. "You may be crazy about dogs, but I'm not. It doesn't mean we can't be friends."

"What about Fifi?" I asked. "You like her, don't you?" Fifi thumped her tail when she heard her name.

Bird patted the poodle on her head. "Yeah, I guess I do."

"Well, what about Clover? She's really a sweet dog. Her problem is that she doesn't get out much. That's why she likes to run."

Shrugging, Bird said, "I guess I could get used to Clover. She's really not so bad. Baby, though, is another story." Bird shuddered.

"Yeah, well, Baby has a lot of growing up to do," I said. "That will help him a lot. Also, the more we work with him, the better he'll get."

"Change the 'we' in your last sentence to 'you.'" Bird shook her head. "I don't think I could ever get used to that dog."

"Not all dogs are like Baby," I said.

"Thank goodness!" Then she surprised me again. "Can I pull the wagon back to Miss Strake's?" she asked shyly.

"Pull away." I handed her the wagon handle and followed her back to Fifi's house.

Miss Strake ran outside to meet us. She hovered and fussed over Fifi. "It looks like the outing did her a world of good. Look at her. My Fifi's smiling!"

Bird scratched Fifi's ears. "She's a good girl."

"Miss Strake," I said, "this is Bernadette." Bird glared at me. "But we all call her Bird," I quickly added. "It was her idea to pull Fifi around in the wagon."

"What a clever girl you are!" Miss Strake exclaimed. "Why, I do believe that Fifi likes you better than Abby." She picked up the poodle and cradled her in her arms. "My little sweetie will want Bird to take her for a walk tomorrow," she cooed.

I said I would be back the next day. As Bird and I walked home, I said, "Miss Strake and Fifi are expecting you to return. Will you?"

"Yeah," Bird said. "I do like that little dog."

I grabbed the opportunity. Maybe this time she'd give me the right answer. "*Now* are you part of the dog-walking service?"

Bird grinned sheepishly. "Fifi thinks I am."

"So do I," I said. "Besides, you're the brains behind this operation. You helped me with each dog. You came up with great solutions for every problem."

"Well—," began Bird.

"You don't have to actually walk the dogs unless you want to," I offered.

Bird burst out laughing. "Do you realize that you haven't really *walked* a single dog?"

I joined her laughter. "You're right! We tricked Baby into following a sandwich. Clover pulled me on skates. And we either carried Fifi or pulled her in the wagon. Some dog-walker I am!"

"You know," Bird said, "you really are good with dogs."

"Thanks," I said. "Growing up with Cody and Winston helped. They were wonderful dogs. You didn't get to have that experience."

"No," Bird replied, "not with my mom's allergies."

"But you have great ideas," I continued. "I don't think I would've 'walked' any of the dogs without your suggestions. You know we'd make a good team."

"Okay," Bird said. "You've convinced me."

"All right!" I shook her hand. "Now I need to tell you about our next customer."

"Doesn't anybody walk their own dog anymore?" Bird asked, pretending to be serious.

"I hope not," I said. "I've got enough money to buy a new chain for my bike. If we keep the dog-walking business going, who knows? Maybe we'll have enough money for new bicycles!"

"I like that idea," Bird agreed. "So who's our newest customer?"

"A Mrs. Webster and her dog, Bear," I said.

"Bear?" Bird looked troubled. "That doesn't sound good. That's the kind of name you give to a mean dog."

"You can't tell by the name," I pointed out. "He's a St. Bernard, and the lady says he's really friendly."

"Let's hope so," said Bird.

"We'll find out together," I said happily.

"Yeah," Bird agreed. "After all, we're the World's Best Dog-Walkers."

We headed for Mrs. Webster's house with the sun shining and us dreaming of new bikes. I looked over at Bird and smiled at her. I'd always heard that a dog is a person's best friend, but now I knew that wasn't true. Bird is the world's best friend.